IMMIGRANT DREAMS

CARO HENRY

KEMODOG
PRESS

For permissions, contact: info@kemodogpress.com

Library of Congress Control Number: 2024925572

Imprint: KemoDog Press

Names: Henry, Caro, author.

Title: Immigrant Dreams / Caro Henry.

Description: Baltimore, MD: KemoDog Press, 2025.

Identifiers: LCCN: 2024925572 | ISBN: 979-8-9914912-4-2 (hardcover) | 979-8-9914912-3-5 (paperback) | 979-8-9914912-5-9 (ebook) | 979-8-9914912-2-8 (kindle) | 979-8-2307792-3-0 (D2D)

Subjects: LCSH American poetry--21st century. | Immigrants--United States--Poetry. | BISAC POETRY / Subjects & Themes / General | POETRY / Subjects & Themes / Animals & Nature | POETRY / Caribbean & Latin American | POETRY / Subjects & Themes / Family | POETRY / Subjects & Themes / Death, Grief, Loss | POETRY / Subjects & Themes / Political & Protest | POETRY / Subjects & Themes / War | POETRY / Women Authors

Classification: LCC PS3608 .E67 I66 2025 | DDC 811.6--dc23

Cover design by Laura Simon

Cover art photo by Caro Henry

First Edition: January 2025

CONTENTS

To those who leave home in search of a better life.

INTRODUCTION

Dreams—hopes, aspirations—weave a thread that binds the past to the present, the familiar to the unknown. *Immigrant Dreams* invites you into the fragile yet resilient world of people, young and old, who have journeyed far from the lands of their birth. Their stories are not just tales of departure; they are rich landscapes of hope, longing, and transformation.

Each poem in this collection captures the essence of those uprooted by necessity—whether fleeing the harsh grip of religious persecution, escaping the suffocating shadows of poverty, or confronting the relentless advance of climate crises. This collection shares the stories of lives carved out of adversity, where dreams dance like candle flames in the darkness of uncertainty.

As these souls navigate the tumultuous waters of change, their dreams become a refuge, a bridge connecting their cherished memories to their aspirations for the future. They dream of sun-drenched fields left behind; laughter shared in familiar tongues, and the warmth of home that now exists only in the recesses of their hearts. In their new lands, they seek survival, a sense of belonging, and a chance to cultivate a new identity that honors their past and journey ahead.

Each thread in the multicolored fabric of life tells a story. The vibrant colors of an immigrant's journey also weave throughout my story. My poems draw from the well of my dreams—dreams that often echo hope, resilience, and the quest for belonging. Each verse reflects my aspirations and the collective yearnings of countless souls who have crossed borders in search of a brighter future. These poems celebrate the struggles and triumphs that define us, capturing the essence of a journey marked by both challenges and the unwavering belief in the possibility of a better tomorrow.

Through my words, I invite you to explore the landscapes of my heart, where dreams take flight against the backdrop of a new world. Reflect on your dreams, recognize the shared humanity that binds us all, and celebrate the rich mosaic of cultures that flourish when we open our hearts to the dreams of others.

EDGAR ALLAN POE

Take this kiss upon the brow!
And, in parting from you now,
Thus much let me avow —
You are not wrong, who deem
That my days have been a dream;
Yet if hope has flown away
In a night, or in a day,
In a vision, or in none,
Is it therefore the less gone?
All that we see or seem
Is but a dream within a dream.

I stand amid the roar
Of a surf-tormented shore,
And I hold within my hand
Grains of the golden sand —
How few! yet how they creep
Through my fingers to the deep,
While I weep — while I weep!
O God! Can I not grasp

Them with a tighter clasp?
O God! can I not save
One from the pitiless wave?
Is all that we see or seem
But a dream within a dream? [1]

1

DREAM COURIERS

The dreams of journeys rise in muted cries,
Across the seas, beneath the endless skies.

With every step, a story left behind,
The weight of home, that's a bond redefined.

They seek the light where shadows seldom
    dwell,
In foreign lands, where their sagas they tell.

With calloused hands, they build a life anew.
Each brick—a testament to their dreams
    pursued.

They gather strength from roots that stretch
    afar,
Embracing cultures like a guiding star.

In markets bright, their laughter fills the air,
A fusion of the spices, bold and rare.

They dream of futures painted in their eyes,
A canvas rich with hopes that touch the skies.

Yet still, the weight of labels lingers near,
A foreign heart, though filled with love and
    cheer.

In crowded streets, their stories intertwine,
A chorus of the brave, a vibrant line.

They carry dreams like lanterns in the night,
Illuminating paths with courage bright.

With every challenge faced, they stand up tall,
For in their hearts, they know they can't be
    small.

The dream of home is not just where they start,
But where they plant their hopes and share
    their heart.

HISTORY'S SHADOW

They come
in the shadow of history,
carrying fragile glass-dreams.
Each suitcase a universe of hope,
laden with bolts of their past—
the laughter of children,
the echo of familiar streets,
the dead weight of longing.

In the cradle of liberty,
where the ink of the Declaration
still whispers in the breeze,
the Founding Fathers carved
dreams into the granite of a new
    world.
Their hopes, like seeds,
scattered across the land, taking
root in fields of ambition, as
ships sailed into the horizon,
carrying souls seeking
    sanctuary.

The Irish, with faces like weathered stone,
fled the specter of withering potato fields,
left behind the cries of the dying,
shattered earth beneath their feet,
the weight of loss heavy in their chests.
So, they arrived in waves,
crossing the ocean, carrying
the scent of damp earth and brine,
dreams not of gold but of fields untouched,
where laughter could rise like bread from the
    oven,
and children could dance with unburdened
    hearts.
Each step forward, a promise of warmth,
each gust of wind, a reminder of home,
their hopes took root in an unfamiliar space,
yearning for a tomorrow brightened by the sun.

Italians, too, crossed the ocean's churning belly,
in the quiet hum of old ships' engines,
bearing the weight of unspoken hopes,
they carried whispers of olive groves,
the scent of tomatoes ripening in the sun,
the aroma of basil and garlic lingering
in their hearts, memories of sunlit fields.
They envisioned bustling streets,
where the air thrummed with laughter,
and doors swung open with warm welcomes,
promising a life unchained from despair.
Each sunrise held a spark of possibility,
an escape from the grip of faded dreams,
far from the shadows of crumbling walls
and the echo of empty stomachs.

And now, the present breathes,
a mosaic of faces from lands near and far,
Guatemalans, Venezuelans, Cubans,
Afghans, Pakistani, Lebanese.
They arrive with stories etched in their eyes,
carrying the weight of their homelands,
where the air is thick with the scent of sorrow,
and the echoes of gunfire linger like ghosts.
In the heart of bustling cities,
they seek refuge in the warmth of new faces,
dreaming of safety wrapped in the framework
     of hope,
where children can play without fear,
and laughter isn't a distant memory.

Each dawn is a canvas painted with possi-
     bilities;
each struggle is a step toward belonging
as they forge paths in the land of dreams,
finding strength in the embrace of the
     unknown.

In the shadows of skyscrapers,
the pulse of America beats;
a cacophony of languages,
an orchestra of dreams,
where each note is a journey,
where every life is a verse;
together, they sing the saga
of a nation built not on solitude,
but on the collective heartbeats
of those who dared to hope,
to venture, to belong.

And so, they gather,
the dreamers and builders,
their narratives entangled
in the ever-evolving story of a nation.
In every corner of this land,
echoes of their journeys resonate,
a symphony of voices
that enriches the essence of existence.

Together, they remind us
that dreams are not solitary,
but collective,
and in the pursuit of better tomorrows,
they forge a legacy,
embroidered with hope
that will endure through generations.

3

BASEBALL HOPES

Where laughter dances with the crack of bats,
in the humid embrace of the Dominican sun,
a young man stands,
wiry silhouette against the azure sky;
his heart a drumbeat of dreams,
echoing through the dusty fields.

With each swing of his bat,
a whisper of possibility;
the wood singing,
melodies of ambition soaring high,
as the ball arcs into the horizon,
a comet of hope.

Then, the call arrives,
a voice through the ether,
Come to the States, it says,
and the world shifts beneath his feet,
the ground a launchpad to destiny,
his family's future tethered to a single moment.

In the new land, fields gleam like emeralds,
the air thick with expectation;
the crack of the bat,
a thunderous applause,
as he steps to the plate,
heart racing, a wild horse unbridled.

The ball zips toward him,
time stretches thin,
a breath held,
then the swing,
the crack resounding like a cannon,
and the ball sails,
a wish released into the universe.

He rounds the bases,
arms raised,
the crowd's roar surrounds him,
a symphony of dreams realized;
each step is a testament to his journey,
of the sacrifices made
under the warm Caribbean sun.

In the field, he is a whirlwind;
a dancer with dirt flying;
each catch a heartbeat,
each dive a prayer.
The thrill of the game ignites his spirit,
the weight of aspirations resting on his
    shoulders.

Challenges rise like mountains;
strikes that sting, losses that haunt;
But he remembers the laughter of friends,
the promise whispered on dusty roads,
and with each setback,
he rises, fueled by resolve,
knowing the major leagues called his name,
a siren song he is destined to follow.

In the twilight of his youth,
with bat in hand and dreams ablaze,
he stands ready,
a warrior in the arena of hopes,
for in every crack of the bat,
he hears the echo of his heart,
the pulse of a future waiting to be claimed.

4

SORROW'S SPRING

Night descends again,
an embrace heavy with
the scent of dry earth.
Sand trickles through her fingers,
warm remnants of a sun long set;
each grain a memory slipping away—
whispers of a Caspian shore,
echoes of water lapping against sand,
gentle caress of twilight breezes,
raucous calls of terns,
migrating shadows against a sky
that feels both distant and near.

But this is the desert,
a lonely, dry expanse,
miles upon miles of
undulating dunes.
Her sister kneels beside her,
urgent fingers grip her arm,
her words slice through the night,

We don't have time to dream!
We have to keep moving!
With that, they rise,
seven figures bound by shared fate,
scarves pulled tight 'round their faces,
eyes wide, reflecting the sliver of moonlight
that dares illuminate their path.

They are a small band of refugees,
each backpack a weight of hope and fear,
guided by a leader,
a man forged in the fires of past journeys,
his gaze hardened by the stark reality—a
world that offers no promises.
He speaks of adventure,
the thrill of the unknown,
a siren's call that lured them
from home's familiarity,
from joyful laughter
echoing through the air
to the blinding sun,
beams diffusing,
filtering hot, sharp tears.

Yet, as they traverse this desolate canvas,
the thrill feels more like a gamble.
Each step is a silent prayer
for safety, for their future;
as dawn approaches,
the village reveals itself—
a mere dozen openings carved
into ancient dunes,
an oasis of hope cloaked in shadows.

Their leader gestures
a silent invitation to the jeep;
the engine's growl promises escape,
metal gleaming with unspoken fears.

They climb aboard,
the world outside fading,
the village swallowed by the expanse,
and her sister's fingers intertwine with hers,
a lifeline in the growing silence.

As they pass two goats,
a memory flits through her mind—
her mother, perched on a wall,
watching another woman milk a goat,
laughter ringing like chimes in the air,
but that joy is a ghost,
fading as gunfire erupts,
the world collapsing into chaos.

Get down!
the leader's voice cuts through,
a command that ignites their fear;
they huddle, bodies pressed together,
hearts thundering as the jeep races forward,
the driver's foot a desperate plea for safety;
and in the mayhem,
she glimpses her mother's face, surprised,
turning toward her father,
a moment suspended in time,
and then darkness swallows her whole.

She wakes, heart pounding;
the dream, a relentless cycle.
A loop of memories,
always returning to the desert,
where hope and despair entwine,
where every grain of sand
holds the weight of her past,
and the horizon stretches endlessly;
a promise of what lies ahead—
a landscape where dreams
sparkle, distant starlight,
a reminder that even in
immense emptiness,
hearts carry echoes of home.

5

HAWK

In the quiet dawn, he dreams of the hawk
    soaring high,
A symbol of freedom, its wings slicing through
    the air,
Reminding him of the home he left, still whis-
    pering its name.

Each flap a promise, each glide a distant
    memory,
He seeks the sky's embrace, a refuge from the
    weight of time.
In its eyes, he sees the strength to rise above, to
    belong.

With each encounter, he learns the language of
    the wind;
The rustle of leaves, the murmur of streams,
Nature's lessons woven into his very being.

He watches the hawk, fierce and unyielding,
As it hunts with purpose, a dance of survival,
Reflecting his own journey, fraught yet
    beautiful.

Memories of Korea flood like the river's flow,
The laughter of family, the taste of home-
    cooked meals,
Yet, in the hawk's flight, he discovers a new
    horizon.

The sky, once daunting, now beckons him
    forward.
Each day, a canvas painted with the hues of
    hope.
He learns to spread his wings, to embrace both
    worlds.

In the hawk's cry, he hears his own voice rising,
Echoing the dreams of countless souls
    before him,
A shared journey, where dreams take flight
    together.

6

BUTTERFLY

A boy on a ship,
waves crashing, salty air,
his family huddles close,
speaking softly of freedom.

Eyes wide, he scans
the endless horizon,
when, a flit of color—
a butterfly, bright.

Dancing on the wind,
a dream of green fields,
laughter in the sun,
far from shadows, terrors.

He imagines a life,
where fear holds no power,
where butterflies linger,
and dreams take flight.

He reaches out,
fingers brushing the breeze,
the butterfly flutters,
soft breaths in the wind.

Night falls, stars awaken,
each twinkle a promise,
the ship rocks gently,
cradling dreams in its arms.

He closes his eyes,
the world fades away,
and his heart drifts
to lands unknown.

With open skies
and endless possibilities,
tomorrow awaits,
where hope blooms anew.

7

BLOSSOMS

She dreams of bridges,
Not of steel, but of understanding.
Her voice is a gentle stream
That seeks to connect,
To unite a world divided.

With each lesson learned,
She gathers words like petals,
Ready to share her culture;
The warmth of her Chinese heritage,
Infused with the essence of tea and tradition.

In the classroom, she listens.
Her eyes wide with wonder
As each story unfolds; every one, a
Thread in the netting of friendship,
Multicolored dreams intersecting.

She dreams of a future
Where language barriers crumble,
Empathy flowers like cherry blossoms.

Her heart's a garden
Where every voice is heard,
And every dream nurtured.
A world painted in unity and peace.

8

TWO WORLDS

I.

Born with golden sun in the Cayman isles,
A titian maiden, her spirit strong, bright,
Her roots entrenched in this land that
      beguiles,
She bloomed beneath the Caribbean's light.

Yet fate had whispered secrets in her ears,
Of ancient tales and stories long ago,
Her ancestors, in Scotland's ancient years,
Their spirit called, and she knew she must go.

So across the oceans, her heart did soar,
To the land where her lineage was enshrined,
In Highland glens, her soul found its restore,
The echoes of her past forever bind.

A woman torn between two worlds she stands,
In Cayman roots, and Scotland's ancient lands.

II.

In Bonnie Scotland, she embraced her clan,
The land of thistles, tartan, and deep lochs,
The bagpipes wailed, her heart danced in
    command,
With every note played, she walked ancient
    docks.

Yet she yearned for her Caymanian shores,
The azure waves, and sands of purest white,
Her childhood memories, forever more,
A beacon shining in her darkest night.

Two worlds collided in her very soul,
A symphony of cultures intertwined,
Her heritage, an oil painting so bold,
Its palette, proof of love's enduring kind.

A woman torn between two worlds she stands,
In Cayman roots, and Scotland's ancient lands.

III.

The Cayman sunsets painted dreams of home,
Where gentle breezes, lulling palm trees sway,
The taste of salt upon her lips did roam,
She longed for these, with every passing day.

Yet Scotland's Highlands whispered tales
    untold,
Of warriors fierce, with kilts and claymores,
Her heart was caught, a story to behold.

In Highland mist, she found her heart and
    more.

Oh, woman of two worlds, your spirit flies,
With Cayman's warmth, and Scotland's ancient
    lore,
A fusion of your essence, reaching skies,
Sure evidence of all that you adore.

A woman torn between two worlds she stands,
In Cayman roots, and Scotland's ancient lands.

IV.

In Cayman's sun-soaked sands, her roots were
    sown,
In Scotland's ancient hills, she found her kin,
A woman of two worlds, she stands alone,
With pride and love, her heart forever spins.

For in her veins, the blood of both doth flow,
A testament to strength, resilience, grace,
A bond unbroken, wherever she may go,
Her spirit shines, a beacon in each place.

So let her dance, with Cayman's golden sun,
And hear the bagpipes' call from Scottish hills,
For in her heart, the twain shall be as one,
A symphony of love that never stills.

A woman torn between two worlds she stands,
In Cayman roots, and Scotland's ancient lands.

9

DREAMS

Dreams coil like vines,
Binding memory to aspiration,
Weaving stories of those uprooted,
Who journey far from familiar shores.

They carry the weight of their past,
Sunlit fields and laughter,
Echoes of home reverberating softly,
Shimmers of hope in shadows of uncertainty.

In new lands, they seek more than survival—
A sanctuary for identity to bloom,
Rich sod for resilience to root,
A bridge between the chasm of loss and
    belonging.

10

WATER RESCUE

A fragile boat sways,
in the cradle of the Timor Sea,
its hull a tired wisp against the roar of waves,
a vessel of dreams and desperation.
He, with hands carved by toil,
stares into the horizon,
where the sun bleeds golden into the water,
each ripple a reminder of home—
Galle, Sri Lanka,
where laughter mingles with the
scent of salt and spices,
where the ocean sang lullabies
and children played in the shadow of palms.

She clutches their children,
the weight of the world in her embrace.
Her heart beats with the rhythm of hope,
each pulse a prayer for safety,
for a future untainted by fear.
In her mind, she dreams of sandy shores,
where school bells ring and laughter echoes,
where her children can run free,
unfettered by the chains of violence.

Their daughter, with star-bright eyes,
leans over the edge,
captivated by the endless blue,
her imagination painting pictures of
    Australia—
a land where sun-kissed beaches stretch,
where the sky is an open door,
inviting them to step into a new life.
Their son, oblivious to the storm brewing,
plays with a frayed rope,
his tiny fingers weaving tales of adventure,
a hero navigating the seas,
unaware of the tempest about to rage.

As clouds gather, dark and heavy,
he feels the storm in his bones,
the engine sputtering like a dying hope,
the weight of their journey pressing down,
a reminder of all they left behind—
the warmth of family, the familiarity of home,
the safety of solid ground.

Then, a distant horn pierces the air,
salvation slicing through despair.
A sturdy vessel emerges,
bold against the chaos,
the Australian Maritime Border Command,
an anchor amidst the turmoil.
Ropes fall like lifelines,
and hope rekindles with each hand extended,
the crew's faces bright with purpose.

One by one, they are lifted,
Their daughter first, a small bird
rescued from the storm,
then his wife with his son,
tears of gratitude mingling with fear,
and finally, he joins them,
looking back to the battered boat,
the dreams that once carried them,
now mere echoes on the water.

As they step onto the deck,
the taste of salt on their lips shifts,
becoming a flavor of promise,
a new life unfolding before them,
and at that moment, they dare to dream
      again—
of laughter ringing in sunlit schools,
parks filled with children's joy,
a future where waves no longer threaten,
but sing of possibility.

11

A BOY'S JOURNEY

In Sudan's heart, where once the sun did gleam,
I ran where laughter floated in the warm air,
But shadows crept and shattered every dream,
As echoes of war turned joy to despair.

With Mother's hand, in darkness we did
    scheme,
To flee the fire, to leave behind our care,
A camp awaited, packed with silent screams,
Where hope grew dim, and sorrow laid us bare.

The scent of sweat and fear hung in the night,
The cries of children filled the heavy gloom,
In endless rows, the tents a woeful sight,
With every heartbeat, whispered tales of doom.

Yet through the dark, a glimmer of pure light,
A chance, a voice, to rise from grief and pain,
An aid that came, like stars that burn so bright,
To lift us from despair and change our bane.

Now France awaits, a land of chance and grace,
Where rivers flow and promise fills the sky,
I long to feel the sun upon my face,
And leave behind the echoes of a cry.

With every step, I dream of a new place,
Where laughter reigns and fears begin to die,
A future bright where I can find my space,
From Sudan's ashes, watch my spirit fly.

With hope reborn, I grasp my mother's hand,
As we embark on paths we've never known,
Each step a prayer, a wish to understand,
The beauty in this world that feels like home.

In fields of green, where children play and
      stand,
I'll tend my dreams, no longer feel alone,
A fertile sward of life, both brave and grand,
In every heartbeat, seeds of love now sown.

The echoes of the past may linger still,
Yet in my heart, the pain will softly fade,
For in this land, I'll learn to climb each hill,
Hear my emotions, music softly played.

With every challenge, I will bob, not spill,
Resilience grows where once my fears paraded.
In France, I'll find my voice, my dreams fulfill,
A bridge of hope, where once dreams cascaded.

So here I stand, a boy under skies so wide,
The sun will rise, its warmth a sweet embrace,
In laughter's light, I'll cast my fears aside,
And dance to rhythms of this new-found place.

With every moment, I will walk with pride,
For from the ashes, I've begun to trace,
A life renewed, where love and dreams collide,
In every heartbeat, I'll find my rightful space.

12

FREEDOM TO LOVE

She walks,
in the quiet corners
of Berlin,
multiple colors
woven in her heart,
each step,
sound waves of dreams,
freedom she craved,
leaving behind
shadows of
whispered threats,
suffocating silence
of a home unwelcoming.

Here,
air tastes of hope,
laughter dances
in the streets,
and love is spoken
in every language,
a vibrant mural
against the gray past;
she finds herself—
unbound, unapologetic.

13

FOREFATHERS

Shadows dance with whispers,
In quiet chambers of night;
Dreams of immigrant forefathers rise,
Woven into the structure of their hopes.

Threaded with the weight of longing,
Each stitch a journey across barren seas;
They stand on the precipice of memory,
Gazing into the fog of yesterday.

The smell of salt and earth mingles,
And the voices of ancestors echo,
Calling them to forge a new path,
Carve their names into foreign dust.

Their dreams are not just fleeting visions,
But a fusion of adaptability and strength,
Painted with hues of struggle and sacrifice,
The laughter of children ringing in the air.

In the distance, a promise whispers,
Of a brighter dawn rising ahead,
Over the horizon of uncertainty,
Where hope and fear intertwine.

In their hearts, a fire ignites,
A fierce desire to belong,
Build homes with hands weathered,
Plant seeds of love in unknown lands.

Transforming clay with stories untold,
Each life a testimony to the dream alive;
Yet in the stillness of the night,
The weight of their dreams lingers on.

Haunting the spaces between breaths,
Reminding us of roads they traveled;
Each step forward a tribute to courage,
A sigh of gratitude to those who dared.

14

GUILT BOMBS

Beneath the ancient oak, he lies,
Green leaves whispering secrets;
The world above, a distant roar,
While echoes of bombs dance in his mind.

Sharp whistles pierce the tranquil air,
Each note a memory of lives shattered;
Friends and family, laughter turned to silence,
Faces sliding by like an old ViewMaster® reel.

Guilt washes over him, a cold tide,
The blue sky, a mocking canvas of peace,
Promising freedom, yet haunted by loss,
The weight of their absence, heavy as stone.

With clenched fists, he grips the earth,
Grass crumpling beneath the pressure of
        sorrow;
Amidst the rustling leaves, he breathes in life,

Earthy scent mingling with the promise of
    renewal.

Each heartbeat a reminder that he remains,
A vessel for their stories, a keeper of their light;
With every passing day, he will carve their
        names
Into the granite of his existence, outlined in
    gold.

He rises, the pull of grief igniting purpose,
The tree, a silent witness to his resolve,
To speak their names, to remember,
Transform guilt into a living tribute.

In the embrace of nature, he finds strength,
The world may tremble, but he will stand firm,
Beneath the sprawling arms of the oak,
He will not forget, he will not let them fade.

15

NO LONG GOODBYES

Leaving;
he couldn't believe it;
the weight of it pressing against him,
a storm cloud looming on the horizon,
threatening to unleash the rain of sorrow.
His father's words,
sharp and solemn,
Your brother is no longer with us,
each syllable a stone dropped into a still pond,
rippling across the surface of his heart.

A small leather satchel,
bound with strips of leather,
rested heavily in his hands,
a fragile anchor in a world turned chaotic.
Hide this money somewhere on your person,
his father had said, urgency laced through his
    tone,
but how could he hide the weight of respon-
    sibility

that pressed down on his young shoulders?
Fifteen years old,
and yet the mantle of adulthood
draped upon him like a cloak
he never asked to wear.

His stomach churned,
a tumult of confusion, fear;
friends left behind,
laughter echoing in empty spaces,
memories fading like dusk.
Nowruz was near,
the air thick with the promise of celebration,
instead, he was bound for the unknown,
a journey into the shadows of uncertainty,
where every step felt like a betrayal
to the vibrant life he had known.

It is best that we do this quickly,
his father's voice, steady yet heavy,
filled the room where plans were made.
Dressed in his favorite pants,
the material soft and worn,
each thread a memory
woven by his mother's hands,
he felt both comforted and exposed,
the loose white shirt, a
borrowed echo of his father,
carrying scents of tobacco and aftershave,
a reminder of safety,
now tinged with the sharpness of loss.

He had tucked away the scarf,
a vibrant piece of cloth,
bright against the muted
palette of his heart;
a symbol of his mother's love,
the warmth of her embrace
folded into each intricate design,
nestled among the remnants of a life
he was forced to leave behind.

Earlier that day,
they had traveled as a family,
the road winding like a ribbon of memories,
from Tehran to Zāhedān,
where orchards stretched out,
sour cherries, pomegranates, figs, apricots,
a cornucopia inviting him to linger,
but now, the sweetness of the fruit
was overshadowed by the
bitterness of departure.

He stood near the doorway,
a sentinel watching,
as his father, uncle, and cousins plotted,
their voices a murmur,
the air thick with anticipation,
while he grappled with the enormity of it all.
Two men entered,
familiar yet distant,
their smiles strained,
promises hanging heavy,
but truth lingered in shadows,

a gnawing sense that friendship could turn to
    dust.

Dinner unfolded,
a feast of laughter and nostalgia,
stories spilling like wine,
the clatter of dishes mingling with
echoes of their past,
but he felt adrift,
lost in a tide of bittersweet memories,
the warmth of their words, a fire
becoming dying embers,
then cold ashes in the night.

Now, they walked past the last row of trees,
the orchard a fading mirage,
the desert stretched ahead, vast and relentless,
an empty canvas waiting for the brushstrokes
of their new reality.
With each step,
the stars blinked into existence,
guardians of his journey,
as he stepped into the darkness,
carrying the weight of his father's dreams,
the legacy of love and loss,
a boy on the brink of becoming,
lost in the vastness of what lay ahead.

16

REMEMBRANCE

Dreams drift through shadows,
In the stillness of night.
Echoes of a past not forgotten,
My grandmother's voice,
Soft and trembling,
Telling tales of a world wrapped in fear.
Streets of Germany,
Once alive with laughter,
Now stifled,
Each corner a reminder
Of neighbors turned strangers.

In hidden basements,
Air thick with dread,
Families gather,
Clutching fragile hopes.

Beneath the weight of a regime,
Whispers of escape routes
Flowed like rivers underground;
Trains slipping through darkness,
Paths winding through forests,
The chill of the night
Biting at their resolve.

Fleeing through shadows,
Some found refuge in France,
Others braved the mountains,
The Pyrenees standing sentinel,
Guardians of freedom,
Each step, a dance with fate—
Fear and courage entwined.

And across the Atlantic,
Ships sailed,
Hulls heavy with dreams.
The Statue of Liberty,
A beacon for the lost,
A promise of safety.
Yet, in my grandmother's eyes,
Faces lingered—
Those who did not escape,
Their stories silenced,
Lives extinguished,
A haunting melody that resonates.

In my heart,
I carry the weight of their trials.
Responsibility weaves through my being,
To honor the resilience of the past.

To remember the stomach-churning hope,
Even in the darkest of nights.
For the legacy of survival
Is embroidered
With threads of courage,
Stories that must be told,
For generations to come.

17

TIME TO EXHALE

The illusion of belonging
dissolves,
in the echo of my voice;
each syllable a passport,
marking me a wanderer
in familiar streets.
Jamaica's warmth,
Wisconsin's chill—
my accent, a filtered melody,
hauntingly nostalgic.

Exhale.

I dream of a world
where my skin does not preface
the story of who I am—
where judgment
is a shadow,
not a spotlight.

Walking through life unburdened,
my presence untainted
by the color of my being.

Exhale.

Imagine stepping into a room,
and the air is rich
with the scent of understanding,
the weight of expectation lifted,
as if intelligence
is a given, not a question.

Exhale.

The liberty of being—
unfiltered, unframed,
existing without the constant
scrutiny of foreign gazes.
A heartfelt release,
like a sigh of relief,
the moment when the world
is just a space to inhabit,
not a stage for performance.

Exhale.

This freedom,
rarely granted to Black and Brown souls
in predominantly white spaces,
is a stolen moment
only found in the embrace

of home or the company
of kindred spirits.
A fleeting taste of anonymity,
a breath of fresh air.

Exhale.

I recall a voice from far away,
an echo from a Caribbean island,
where skin color is not an identity
but a simple fact of life—
no definitions, no boundaries.

Exhale.

Anonymity,
a balm for weary spirits,
the grace of not being seen
through the lens of judgment.
In these moments,
I am unremarkable,
and in that, I find strength.
No longer carrying the weight
of white strangers' eyes,
no longer feeling diminished
by the force of their gaze.

Exhale.

And now,
in this space I call home,
I inhale deeply,
grateful for the freedom
to simply be.

18

IN SITU

He sits with a notebook,
ink smudged on his fingers,
from the cheap ballpoint,
his thoughts sifting, riffing.

He dreams of crafting tales,
of complex yet relatable characters,
their lives rich
with the history
he carries in his bones.

With every word,
he explores the landscapes of his mind,
a world in situ, fossilized,
the rolling hills, the ancient stones,
where legends linger in the mist.

In class,
he shares stories.
His voice,
a Celtic melody,
a bridge to the past,
where he finds solace
in the rhythm of language.
Each lesson, a stepping stone
toward the worlds he wishes to create.

His dreams echo in his friends' laughter,
as they inspire each other to soar.

19

NO SAFE REFUGE

In shadows deep where whispers coil and
    creep,
A girl finds solace in her brother's gaze,
While dreams of home and hope begin to seep.

The camp surrounds, where silence dares to
    leap,
She feels the weight of eyes in the night's haze,
In shadows deep where whispers coil and
    creep.

His arms a fortress, strong and wide, they keep
The men at bay, their hearts a maze,
While dreams of home and hope begin to seep.

She drifts through memories, a gentle sweep,
Of laughter, light, and sunlit summer days,
In shadows deep where whispers coil and
    creep.

Her dreams are painted with the colors steep,
Of futures bright, where fear no longer plays,
While dreams of home and hope begin to seep.

Together, silent oaths they vow to reap,
Guardians of each other in this phase,
In shadows deep where whispers coil and
    creep,
While dreams of home and hope begin to seep.

20

LEAVING

The old Peugeot raced,
Maryam's heart kept pace,
a wild song of fear and hope,
her dreams cradled in a worn bag,
clutching her hijab,
a fragile shield against the storm outside.

Tehran's streets blurred,
voices of the city fading,
her own voice ringing loud,
echoing with defiance,
but shadows loomed,
threatening her family,
her father's sacrifice—
Fadat besham!
a bittersweet refrain of love.

On a dirt road, uncertainty twisted,
the driver spoke of safety,
yet her heart trembled,
as a bearded man opened the door,
offering refuge,
silence heavy in the air,
the weight of shared fears.

Days turned into nights,
listening to distant news,
waiting for a chance,
the pulse of freedom quickening.
A Saipa sedan, old but resolute,
her ticket to the border,
where hope flickered like a distant star.

But the road twisted,
military trucks—dark sentinels,
each turn deepening her despair,
until a wiry man emerged,
his voice a gruff promise.

Through fields and darkness,
each step a prayer,
blisters blooming on her feet,
yet she pressed on,
the dream of escape burning bright.
At the border, mountains loomed,
a narrow path beckoning,
her heart a vessel of gratitude,
tears streaming as
she whispered her thanks,
before embarking into the unknown.

With every step,
the weight of Iran fell behind,
her spirit soared toward freedom,
a life woven with dreams,
where the sun kissed the horizon,
and hope danced in the air,
unbound and unbroken,
Maryam walked onward to a life
where her voice could sing,
untethered.

21

MOTHER'S DREAMS

Quiet night,
hopeful whispers,
drifting softly,
feathers,
carried on winds
to distant shores.

Eyes closed tight
she sees
futures,
painted in colors,
unfamiliar yet bright;
stars igniting,
in a midnight sky,
each gleam a promise.

Hands worn
from labor,
hold dreams gently,
fragile glass,
shimmering in sunlight;
the weight of love,
ever so heavy.

Little feet,
treading paths,
unknown and wide,
worn by journeys,
of sacrifice;
quiet strength,
etched in her heart.

Every tear shed,
a seed planted,
in earth rich
with resilience;
nurtured by stories,
of ancestors lost,
but never forgotten.

With each dawn,
she inhales the
scent of possibility;
it fills the air,
as she dreams
of laughter echoing,
through open doors.

Her voice a melody,
soothing and soft,
murmurs of courage
to chase light;
for her children,
the world awaits,
arms wide open.

22

THE SPIRIT'S LONGING

I.

When dawn arose, the compound stood still,
A place where joy trilled in the morning air.
Yet tremors shook the ground, a nation's will,
With heavy hearts, they left, a burdened care.

The missionaries, her own family,
Were forced to flee the chaos drawing near.
With words of prayer they tried to make
    her see,
They had to leave behind their loved ones
    there.

In distant lands, the memories remain,
The spices of her homeland haunt her dreams.
The vibrant streets, now shadowed by her pain,
The laughter lost, yet still in silence beams.

In every tear, she holds her past so tight,

A thread that twists through darkness into
    light.

II.

Yet in her heart, the spirit still ignites,
A dance of faith that mingles with the past.
In every prayer, she finds her soul takes flight,
And in the silence, dreams are held steadfast.

The voices of her people call her home,
Their songs entwined with whispers of the
    night.
In foreign lands, she feels the need to roam,
To find the pieces lost, to seek the light.

Among the strangers, kindness starts to bloom,
A shared existence woven through their hands.
Each meal prepared dispels a hint of gloom,
A bridge between the worlds, where hope
    expands.

Though distance stretches far across the sea,
In every heart, she finds her family.

III.

In gatherings beneath the starlit sky,
They share their stories, laughter, and their
    tears.
With every tale, she learns to say goodbye,
Yet holds the threads of love that span the
    years.

The flavors of her home dance on her tongue,
Each dish a tribute to the life she knew.
In kitchens filled with warmth, the songs are
    sung,
A celebration of the past, so true.

Though echoes of her land grow faint with
    time,
The rhythm of her heart beats strong and clear.
Through every prayer, she finds a way to climb,
To rise above the weight of doubt and fear.

In unity, their spirits lift and shine,
A merger of hope that will not decline.

IV.

Yet still, she dreams of Haiti's sunlit shores,
To walk the streets where history is sown.
To feel the love that on her heart restores,
A longing deep, a seed of hope that's grown.

In every breath, the ocean's whispers call,
To witness life where colors brightly play.
The laughter of her people, a sweet thrall,
In every heartbeat, memories hold sway.

Until that day, she carries Haiti's flame,
A light that shimmers softly in the dark.
Though distance stands, her heart will never
    blame,
For in her soul, the spirit leaves its mark.

With every step, she knows she'll find a way,
To bridge the gap, and greet a brand new day.

23

FANNING

In the vast stillness of the sunlit room,
The fans hum low, cool whispers in her ear,
Their blades slice through the air, a gentle
    dance,
Like memories that flutter in her mind.

She dreams of fields where golden grains do
    sway,
Of laughter shared beneath a vast blue sky,
Each gust a brush of hope against her skin,
A promise whispered in the language lost.

Her heart, a boat adrift on tides of time,
Navigates the wild currents of her past,
While shadows play upon the faded walls,
Reminders of a life left far behind.

In daydreams spun by currents soft and free,
She finds her strength, her voice, her destiny.

24

NIGHT HORRORS

He slips into his dreams, in shadows deep,
As his memory's weight presses on his heart.

Familiar streets now haunted by their past,
Their colors fade to gray; hope is lost to fear.

He runs through alleys, breathless and alone,
Where children's laughter twisted into screams.

His mother calls to him, an urgent plea,
Hide quickly now, they come for you, my son!

The men in masks emerge with eyes of stone,
Their voices low, they know just where he
    hides.

Each footfall echoes like the beat of drums,
A march of fear that rattles through his bones.

He stumbles back, trapped in a web of dread,

The faces of the lost rise from the dark.

Gunshots pierce the silence, sharp and cruel,
The scent of smoke and blood wraps 'round his
    throat.

He sinks into a pit of endless night,
Where ghosts of those he loved reach out
        for him.

The morning light creeps slowly through the
    blinds,
But shadows linger still, a heavy shroud.

In silence, he confronts the pain of loss,
The country he fled echoes in his mind.

Escape was more than leaving all behind,
Its battles were fought within the heart and
        soul.

Yet hope remains, a shimmer in the dark,
A fragile spark that dares to seek the dawn.

Each day, he rises, burdened yet alive,
With dreams of freedom whispering his name.

The path ahead is paved with scars and tears,
But in his heart, he knows he must move on.

25

TO BE OR NOT TO BE

I am a tempest in a teacup,
swirling in the confines of life
unraveled by the weight of expectation,
the shadows of dreams whispering
in a language I can't grasp.

I should be married already!
My heart thunders,
a rebel against the chains
of duty and the clinking of dishes,
the aroma of saffron and rose water
drifting ghost-like through the halls.

My father's apprentice,
with dark eyes that hold the sun,
clicks and clacks through my mind,
a fleeting spark that ignites
a world of imagined touches,
the brush of fingers,
first accidental, then electric—
a dance of possibility,
unseen yet achingly real.

But now, the dream
fades like the afternoon light,
dimming under the weight of reality,
for my parents have spoken—
the finality in their words,
a pact drawn in the ink of fear.

How can they tear me from this place?
This sanctuary of cool marble beneath my feet,
the laughter echoing through the air,
the sweet zoolbias,
sugar syrup clinging to my tongue,
the taste of home woven into my being.

Unfair! I shouted,
the word, a wildflower in a storm.
I stood defiant, a pillar of fury,
but the sadness in my father's eyes
cut deeper than any blade.
Please, he whispered,
a prayer wrapped in sorrow,
We do this to save you.

His hands, once a fortress,
slipped from my grasp,
and I stormed away,
my footsteps heavy with betrayal,
each step a crack in the foundation
of all I held dear.

The next day,
the sun rose again,
but it was a different light,
a stranger that washed over me,

and I found myself
in the shadow of my uncle's house,
Urmia welcoming me
with its arms open yet foreign,
a world where laughter might linger
but would never be my own.

And in the quiet corners of my mind,
I wonder,
to be, or not to be—
a question with no answer,
only the ache of what was,
and what could have been,
echoing through
the chambers of my heart.

26

LOST DREAMS

A world jousting with itself,
As lances strike blows at stories, Questioning—
truth or fiction?

Have you tasted the ash of lost dreams,
Heard the crack of promises unkept,
Felt their weight,
A stone tethered to your tongue,
Each foreign word a struggle to articulate?

Did you clench your fists,
Stare ahead with steely eyes—
Instead of bowing your head,
A supplicant to corrupt power—
Your salty tears glistening
With hope and determination?

A mirror split into spidery veins,
Reflecting fragments of home;
Kintsugi-patched with golden
Memories seamed with beauty.
Yet that same mirror blocks your path,
A barrier to understanding,
To belonging,
To a place that feels like yours.

27

A SAILOR'S YEARNING

On quiet nights, the old man drifts away,
His dreams afloat on ships of distant pasts,
A sailor's heart still yearning for the bay.

He crossed the ocean, bold, beneath the gray.
A canvas stretched with hopes that held him
    fast.
On quiet nights, the old man drifts away.

The Navy called, through storms, he found
    his way,
Each battle etched in shadows long amassed,
A sailor's heart still yearning for the bay.

From foreign shores, where echoes of men lay,
He wore the stars, the honor unsurpassed,
On quiet nights, the old man drifts away.

CARO HENRY

A citizen of lands both bright and fray,
With stories woven deep, his voice steadfast,
A sailor's heart still yearning for the bay.

Now, at a century, he finds the sway
Of memories like tides, they come and cast,
On quiet nights, the old man drifts away,
A sailor's heart still yearning for the bay.

28

AN ARTIST'S CANVAS

Each night, she dreams of laughter
mingling with the scent of spices
in the heart of the bustling souk,
her fingers stained with the colors of her
    palette,
as her canvases stretch wide.

With each brush stroke,
she paints her dreams into existence:
a world alive with stories,
each hue a whisper of her Moroccan heritage.

Each night, she dreams of galleries,
where her art breathes,
where the echoes of her ancestors resonate,
and the sun-drenched streets
come alive under her brush.

With every lesson in English,
she learns to express her soul,
to translate the rhythm of her heart
into a language that transcends borders;
her spirit dancing between cultures,
silken threads of hope;
her dreams shimmering in starry skies
over the Atlas Mountains.

29

REVIVAL

She sits on the worn porch,
in the stillness of the night,
the wood creaking beneath her,
a reminder of the weight she carries.
The air is laced with the scent of earth,
damp from the rain,
and whispers of bonfires
crackling in the distance,
a symphony of normalcy
that feels both foreign and comforting.

She closes her eyes,
and the memories flood in—
the hurricane's feral roar,
the sky turning angry,
the ocean swallowing her home whole,
palm trees bending, twisting,
dancers caught in a storm,
their vibrant greens reduced to splinters.

A nightmare of wreckage:
splintered wood and shattered glass,
her life turned inside out,
and the ghosts of laughter
echoing in the empty rooms
where sunlight once poured in
like golden honey.

And yet, amid the ruins,
there is her daughter,
wild curls bouncing,
eyes wide with wonder,
spinning in circles on the porch,
a princess in her own kingdom,
unaware of the shadows
that   sometimes   linger
behind her mother's smile.

Each morning,
she watches her daughter
stride toward the bright kindergarten,
a backpack swaying like a buoy,
each step a defiance against the past,
and her heart swells
with hope, tiny dewdrops
clinging to petals of new
blooms.

In the café,
the warmth of coffee envelops her,
the laughter of customers
mingling with the aroma,
and with every cup she serves,
a piece of her heart
stitches itself back together,
a quilt of kindness,
a patchwork of strangers turned friends.

But when night falls,
the past returns—
the hurricane's song
haunting her dreams,
a lullaby woven with fear.
And she wakes,
her breath a stone caught in her throat,
as she feels the pull of memories,
the weight of loss lingering like a fog.

Yet she dreams anew,
of fields stretching into infinity,
where her daughter runs,
her laughter a melody of freedom,
where the seasons paint their lives
in vibrant hues—
fiery reds of autumn,
gentle whites of winter,
hopeful greens of spring,
colorful flowers of summer.

She dreams of a table
set for Sunday dinners,
surrounded by warmth and light,
stories shared like bread,
memories rising like dough,
and in that vision,
she finds the strength to rise,
to create a life of resilience,
to plant roots in this new soil.

With each passing day,
she nurtures her dreams,
tending to them like seedlings.
Together,
they will grow—
stronger than the winds
that sought to tear them apart.
A bright quilt of hope,
woven from laughter, love,
and unyielding determination.
One step,
one dream,
one day at a time.

30

STITCHES

Where the river once murmured,
near the village of Chamba,
the rains came like an avalanche,
devouring dreams, homes, and laughter.

She stood, heart pounding,
the world dissolving into chaos,
a chorus of voices urging her,
Run, child, flee the rising tide.

With nothing but the clothes she wore,
she sprinted through fields turned to lakes,
her breath a wild wind,
her heart a fierce drum echoing loss.

Days blurred into nights of struggle,
ghosts of laughter and spice haunting,
but hope sparked in her chest,
a tiny flame against the storm.

With the weight of her past,
she boarded a plane to Italy,
each mile a stitch in her journey,
each breath a prayer for a new beginning.

In the bustling workshop,
textiles softly sang tales of elegance,
her fingers danced with determination,
stitching dreams into reality.

Language was a barrier,
but her heart spoke in colors,
each thread a bridge to the future,
every design a testament to her will.

Then came Luca, laughter like sunlight,
in the warmth of shared meals,
love blossomed like flowers in spring,
binding their souls, their fates.

In the heart of Milan,
her creations graced the runways,
a celebration of resilience,
a song of survival sung through fabric.

By the window, she watched sunsets,
the sky painted in gold and crimson,
and though the village was distant,
its spirit thrummed within her.

No longer a survivor,
but a creator, an artist,

each stitch a story of loss and love,
of dreams sewn together, radiant and bold.

31

C'È UN PO' DI MAGIA

.

Footsteps echo,
on foreign land;
hearts heavy,
with hope.

C'è un po'
di magia in
ognuno di noi *
breathed in silence.

Eyes searching,
for the familiar,
in strange faces,
distant lands.

---

* There is a bit of magic in each of us.

Winds carry,
stories untold,
the rhythm of
new beginnings.

Voices rise,
in unison,
melodies of,
longing and love.

Courage flares,
candles,
lighting the path
to tomorrow.

Each heartbeat,
a promise
of dreams alive,
in the night.

Together we soar,
on fragile wings;
finding home
in the journey.

32

FALLING

He stood at the precipice of reality,
breath caught in the tangled web of his throat,
the world around him, a blur of motion and
    stillness—
as if time had become a reluctant companion,
creeping, crawling—
each second stretched like an ancient elastic
    band,
ready to snap.

A leaf, delicate and trembling, brushed his
    cheek,
a soft caress from the autumn air,
its journey downward a whisper of inevitability.

He closed his eyes, surrendering to the
    symphony of nature,
the rustling orchestra of falling leaves,
each one a gentle sigh,
a final farewell to the branches that had held
    them,
now bare against the cobalt sky.

In this cocoon of darkness,
he listened intently,
the wind, a soft voice,
a storyteller shaking free the remnants of
    summer,
inviting him into the fold of a deeper silence,
one he had never known yet yearned to
    embrace.

He wanted to open his eyes, to shatter the spell,
but the weight of the moment held him captive,
a prisoner of his own body,
where the pulse of life began to falter,
and pain curled around his heart like a vine.

In the depths of his mind,
a vivid scene unfurled,
his mother on a sandy shore,
her silhouette framed by a cerulean expanse,
the sea a shimmering glass, undulating gently.
She stood, a figure of warmth,
her back turned, gazing into the horizon,
where the sun kissed the water goodnight.

He reached out, fingers trembling,
the desperate need to connect,
to touch the softness of her shoulder,
to feel the love that had once wrapped
    around him,
a warm blanket on a winter's night.

One last breath,
heavy with the weight of unspoken words,
his heart pounding like a drum,
and then—
she turned,
a smile breaking across her face,
radiant as the dawn,
I'm here, Mama, he thought,
the words floating, feather-like
in the vast emptiness of his fading
consciousness.

And as she enveloped him in her
embrace, the world melted away,
the sounds of rustling leaves replaced by
the lullaby of the sea, and in that
moment,
he knew he was home.

33

IMMIGRANT DREAMS

She cradles her teacup,
in the hush of dawn,
the steam spiraling upward,
like her dreams escaping the
confines of yesterday.
She sits on the balcony, a patch of concrete
overlooking a city that never sleeps,
where the sun rises reluctantly,
as if unsure whether to illuminate the shadows
that linger in the corners of her heart.

Memories rush in, a tidal wave of color—
the cerulean of Caribbean seas,
the vibrant laughter of friends,
the sweet aroma of spices wafting through
    the air,
each recollection a note in the symphony of her
    past.
She can almost hear the rhythm of the waves,
the pulse of a life once lived under golden skies,
where dreams felt like promises whispered by
    the wind.

But here, in this foreign land,
the horizon is painted with a different brush,
one dipped in shades of doubt and fear.
College halls echo with knowledge,
but the specter of solitude haunts her steps,
a ghost of a love that crumbled
like dry leaves underfoot.

His smile, once a lighthouse,
now blinks, a dying bulb,
and their vows dissolve into the air,
leaving only a gossamer strand
of what could have been.
Their radiant daughter,
is a bloom in the cracks of concrete,
her laughter, a melody that cuts through the
    silence.
Her mother, a gardener tending to her dreams,
waters the roots of resilience with hope.

Yet the world outside is a canvas of prejudice,
each glance a brushstroke of scorn,
each word a jagged stone,
and she learns to wear her skin like armor,
a shield against the arrows of ignorance.
She walks through grocery aisles,
where whispers curl like smoke,
and stares pierce like thorns,
but she stands tall, a willow in the storm,
her spirit bending but never breaking.

At night, when the city hums a lullaby,
she pulls out her used textbooks,
the pages worn, dog-eared, stained with
    ambition.
By the soft glow of a lamp, she studies,
the glint of light illuminating her dreams,
her heart swelling with the promise of
    tomorrow.
Each line she reads is a step toward the horizon,
each word, a brick in the foundation of her
    future.

Her daughter grows, a phoenix rising,
her dreams stretching wide like the sky,
unfurling, wings ready for flight.
They share their hopes beneath the stars,
the cosmos, a sail for their aspirations;
the bond between them, a canvas of love
painted with colors of strength and under-
    standing.

Together, they navigate the currents of life,
their dreams woven like roots of an ancient
    tree,
grounded in the loam of survivorship,
reaching for the sun,
unfazed by the storms that threaten to shake
    them.

She dreams of a practice,
a haven where hearts can heal,
her hands guiding others toward light—
a lighthouse for lost souls.

And in quiet moments,
as the sun dips below the horizon,
she envisions a future painted in warm hues—
laughter echoing through their home,
the soft breeze whispering promises,
and the tides of hope rising with the moon,
forever relentless,
forever illuminating the path of their dreams.

NOTES

EDGAR ALLAN POE

1. Copyright Credit: Edgar Allan Poe, "A Dream Within a Dream" from The Works of the Late Edgar Allan Poe, ed. R. W. Griswold. New York: J. S. Redfield, 1850. Public Domain.

ACKNOWLEDGMENTS

1. Written Tales Magazine can be found at https://www.writtentales.com/ & https://writtentales.substack.com/.

ACKNOWLEDGMENTS

Acknowledgment is due to the following for their support:

Many thanks to Kris Diaz and Stephanie Hait, my first readers, for their generosity of spirit, time, and dedication.

Thanks to the talented Laura Simon for using a photo I took while on vacation at Bethany Beach, Delaware, and transforming it into a spectacular cover.

I want to thank Kevin of Written Tales magazine[1] for his editing and publishing help and expertise.

Many thanks to all who support me by reading my work on my website.

As always, I could not have accomplished this without my husband's love and support. His encouragement means the world to me.

ABOUT THE AUTHOR

Caro Henry, a Caribbean American, has a natural bond with the rhythmic soul of the Caribbean. The soulful beats of the islands, along with the harmonious tunes of reggae music and the colorful tapestry of the native patois of Jamaica and the Cayman Islands, influenced her upbringing. Caro's passion for poetry and storytelling flourished as she grew up in tight-knit Jamaican and Cayman Island communities that cherished them. As Caro adjusted from her Caribbean upbringing to life in America, she found solace in writing, using poetry and short stories to bridge the gap between her past and present.

Caro lives in a Maryland suburb of Washington, DC, with her husband and dog. Besides writing, she tends to her garden and creates a welcoming environment for all the critters (domesticated and wild) that call her yard home. Through her website (https://www.caroehenry.com), she distributes her poetry and stories to the world.